Optimism in the Face of Death

A Somalian success story

AHMED EGAG

authorHOUSE®

AuthorHouse™
1663 Liberty Drive, Suite 200
Bloomington, IN 47403
www.authorhouse.com
Phone: 1-800-839-8640

First published by AuthorHouse   6/12/2008

ISBN: 978-1-4343-9330-2 (sc)

Printed in the United States of America
Bloomington, Indiana

This book is printed on acid-free paper.

Dedication;

I'd like to dedicate this book to my son and daughter, Salah and Siham; you are my pearl and diamond. While there have been many joys in my life, I can honestly say that there has never been any greater happiness than seeing my own flesh and blood playing, laughing and sleeping in peace.

Introduction

Optimism in the face of death is the success story of Ahmed Mohamoud Egag. The book does not focus so much on the politics of the War; rather this is a story about the importance of, and rewards that result from remaining optimistic during the bleakest of times. In fact, being too young to of been embedded into any tribal politics, this was probably what allowed Ahmed to consider options other than those few obvious choices that ended up costing so many others their lives.

Ahmed was living in Mogadishu when the war broke out. The story's he documents will move your heart, and how he survives should inspire and motivate all. His humbleness, his patience, his perseverance, this is the story of power of a positive attitude and it can not be overstressed particularly for those still very much struggling for success.

Of course most Somali's will be able to relate to his testimony as well as to the few scenes from the war that he does talk about. Himself only fourteen years old when the violence in Mogadishu broke out, Ahmed gives you an unbiased look at what war and success are all about.

Lastly, there is an importance in the role model Ahmed offers to African youth struggling with identity. Surely the Somalian community is aware of the trends and vices consuming their youths. Ahmed is a great example of the possibilities that await those brave enough to sidestep the vices and all the negative media and propaganda that has influenced so many black peoples perception of themselves and there for their destructive behaviors.

So, sit back and prepare for the journey. Prepare for the inspiration.

I don't know what *you* were doing in 1990 but those of us in Somalia were anticipating the rebellion that had already engulfed most of the country and would soon be closing in on the capitol city, Mogadishu, my nations Capital, the birth place of African worriers. For months prior it had been the talk of the town but having not actually happened yet, we had no choice but to go on living our lives as we had been.

I remember it being a partially cloudy afternoon on what started out to be a typically casual day. People were out walking around, driving to and fro, just taking care of their usual everyday business. I was lying in my bed reading over my ninth grade mid-term test results when all of a sudden- BOOM! An explosion like I've never heard had just rocked the city. It didn't take long before the word got around that, as had been anticipated, the rebellion had finally reached Mogadishu. Panic, fear and sadness instantly overcame the city. Those more mature were worried about the unpredictability of what might happen next, the safety of their relatives' and the future of their children. Those youth's who were too young to comprehend the seriousness of the situation, they were just glad knowing there would be no school tomorrow.

Within the next couple of days the city of Mogadishu had become unfamiliar to even those of us who had been living there all of our lives. All the street lights were out. There was no electricity, no running water, and seeing three, four or more dead bodies lying on the sidewalk in groups, these scenes became so common-place that you had to move around like it was all just part of the landscape. Gun shots were going off all day and all night. Robberies and raping were rampant, all this was going on in one of the most historic cities in east Africa if not throughout the whole continent, now embroiled in a chaos that has been brewing for some fifteen years and finally spilling over into the city of Mogadishu.

The intentions of the rebels were unclear to many of us and so, we, the citizens of Mogadishu, felt as if we had no choice but to flee south to the city of Kismayo. Of course there were also many people who believed that the rebels 'cause' justified their means. They believed, as did many other tribes, that the ruling president of 21 years, Mohamed Siad Bare had begun to run a dictatorship. Some tribal peoples saw the rebels as their liberators and so, in support, chose to stay put in Mogadishu. Many would pay dearly for their miscalculation.

Many Somalian historicists will tell you that Mohamed Siad Bare had done a very good job during the first ten years of his presidency. He had roads built, hospitals, schools and jobs were created, and the economy had improved dramatically! Also Somalia's dealings with other countries and with their leaders, these relationships were as good as anyone could have ever wished for. If you would have asked any ordinary Somali how the president was doing during the early years of Bares reign, they would have told you "Long live our beloved president". And while most of us are unable to relate to being a president of a country for 21 years, we all can relate to Mohamed Siad Bare's humanness" of having made a bad decision. How many of us have lost jobs, careers, loved ones and maybe worse because of a bad decision. It seems to be a general consensus amongst most Somalis that the war Bare brought to Ethiopia in 1977 was in fact that one bad decision which led to the end Bares 21 year rule and his eventual exile.

My family hung around Mogadishu for about a week after the explosion before we decided to follow the thousands of civilians who had already left. We packed the little things we could and started heading towards southern Somalia. Of course we were not alone. The streets were jammed with cars, pick-up's and cargo trucks, everybody was running from the chaos and the senseless killings taking place and none of us knew how long the fighting was going to go on, nor did any of us know what we were going to do once we got to Kismayo.

We drove three days straight before we felt safe enough to unpack and get some rest. Kismayo was some 500 km from the capital city of Mogadishu. I had never been there, although I've always heard that it was a rich city with very creative and hard working people.

The city actually had a lot to offer both the natural citizens and those of us refugees coming from Mogadishu. Yet it was not hard to see the misconceptions and the barriers that came between the Native born Kismanyo and us refugees. They understood we were in a crisis but they made sure to keep their distance from us.

In many respects Kismayo was no different than Mogadishu. People possessed guns like they did shoes. You could look anywhere and you'd see guns mounted up on pick up trucks that were carrying guys holding M16s and AK 47's. With ammunition wrapped around their shoulders, they were looking like black Rambo's starving for action. Gun shots and hand grenades were going off everywhere. People were getting killed in large numbers regardless of his or her tribal affiliation. Defenseless citizens would be stopped by someone toting a gun and would be asked *"are you for the rebels or the government"*. One often had no idea if they were being asked by a rebel or a government supporter and the wrong answer got you shot immediately and with no remorse. I think we were being written off by the thugs who were running the city into the ground. In fact they would kill you just to make robbing you easier.

Most of people that I saw had been killed with seemingly one gun shot. By the way their bodies were lying on the ground you could tell how they had re-acted to their killers just seconds before their last breath.

One March afternoon in 1991 still remains fresh in my memory to this very today. Three men had walked right past me and two of my friends. Two of the guys were holding AK47's and they seemed to be escorting the third man. The sight was so common place that we didn't give it a second thought. A few minutes later we heard "Pump! Pump! Pump!" gun shots! Immediately we turned around and our eyes caught the defenseless man as he hit the ground. The two armed men were fast walking away from their crime.

Many people came out and formed a large circle around the dying man. There was nothing anyone could do to help him. All anyone could do was watch him die a painful and slow death. He began chocking on his own blood; his eyes suddenly rolled back in his head. Still fighting for breath you could hear what sounded like a deep snoring. Seconds later it was more than obvious to all watching that the man had died lying there in a pool of his own blood. This is one of the many images I try to keep locked up somewhere in the back of my head which is not easy in this war torn era of ours where death is sensationalized. What bothered me the most at the time was that no one was asking why the man was shot to death? What did he do wrong?

On April 1991, General Mohamed Farah Aided and his thugs had once again defeated the Darood clan and have now overtaken the city of Kismayo only this time we were taken totally by surprise. And just as in Mogadishu, we started fleeing again.

There was only one road that led out of the city which made for more chaos. Imagine thousands and thousand of cars were on this one lane country dirt road and everyone was trying to be the first one out. I jumped on the first passing truck I could. I had no idea who the people in the truck were. Neither did they know me and my presence immediately caused a heated argument over whether or not they should let me ride with them. There was an older guy on the truck who tried to push me off the moving vehicle but I had a *strong* grip and I wasn't about to let it go for *no*-body. After a couple of failed attempts, thank god, he eventually left me alone. I reluctantly took my eyes off of them for a few seconds to look back and see the beautiful city of Kismayo disappear from sight.

To aggravate our plight it was the rainy season. People were desperate and panicking, the roads were jammed with cars, some of which were abandoned because they had gotten stuck in the mud. It was absolute chaos. After spending most of the day in traffic we eventually came to a grinding halt as the roads became to muddied for any further travel. As we began to get out of our cars it soon became apparent where we would be spending the night so, we resigned to the fetching of water and the making of stone fires for tea.

As the night ensued so did our fears. The roaring of the lions and the heckling of hyenas are anticipated in the jungle and the thought of snakes would make for a long bleak and sleepless night.

The family that I had hitched a ride with consisted of nine people. There was the father and mother, their three daughters, their elder son and his wife and her two younger brothers. Their second oldest daughter was stunningly beautiful. She was slender and tall with beautiful dark brown skin. Her long dark curly hair was breath taking.

She had my attention from the first time I laid my eyes on her. Every now and then I had to pinch myself to keep my focus on the reality at hand. The mother was aware of my attraction to her daughter although she hardly seemed impressed by me. She didn't put that in words but her body language said it all. However, I carried on and did what I had to do in order to survive this disaster. And while this family weren't two thrilled about me being there they did seem to enjoy the taste of my tea. Thank the Lord, we made it another day.

Not long after the sun had risen the cars had started moving again. Me and my new found family gathered up our belongings, got in the vehicle and started rolling. We traveled throughout the morning passing body parts all along the way. A leg here, an arm and head over there. From time to time we would see a full human body on the side of the road lying in a pool of blood. There were people who had gotten stuck in the mud and because everyone was in a desperate panic to get out, those with legs and waist stuck in the mud were left behind and one could only imagine what fate these people faced when the sun went down, Lions, Hyena's, e.t.c.

We all saw these unpleasant scenes and it made for a long eerie trip. I could hear the father and his wife carrying on as if they were completely unbothered by all the gore we were witnessing. Maybe they were trying to be strong for their children so they hid their emotion as to avoid creating any more panic. I imagined that deep down in their thoughts they were questioning what the Gods intentions were in all this.

One afternoon their eldest daughter reached a boiling point as she just could not take it any longer. She got sick and began throwing up. Then she started screaming saying *"I want to die, please God, take me, take me now and go on."* Then she started throwing up again. I sympathized with her because I was in pain myself. Nevertheless, the last thing I wanted was to die. In fact, I had every intention of surviving and was too hungry to wish death on myself or anyone for that matter. I still had dreams I want to accomplish and I looked forward to being a father some day.

Three days into our journey we still hadn't reached the boarder between Somalia and Kenya. Had there been some modern roads this journey would have only taken maybe 10 hours or less. As darkness moved in on the third night, the road conditions grew worse. Eventually an old man near the front of the pack, he had decided to put his car in park for the night. Because no one could drive around him we all had to stop.

Whenever we stopped for a few hours or overnight, everyone was expected to help out in one way or another. On one particular night I decided to go collect some fire wood. I must have been really of kilter as I would spend quite a bit of time searching before I would realize that I was never going to find any dry wood because it had been raining almost all day. Nevertheless I was determined to help and so I continued my search loosing track of time as I had no watch. Finally, after collecting the few pieces that I could, I would go back to the family only to discover that they had already cooked white steamed rice ate it all before I got back.

Many of us had taken the roads to exit the city, but other people were jumping on boats that were already overcrowded. They were attempting to reach Mombasa, Kenya by sea. There was one tragic accident that will forever remain in the minds and hearts of all us who were there and had survived that war. One of the boats had become so crowded by the hundreds of panicking refugees that it would eventually capsize. Dozens of people had died as a result of this incident and some individuals were left as the sole survivor of their heirs. The story rippled across the Somali community as everyone seemed to know or was related to someone on that boat.

Years later I would meet an elderly woman who with her daughters, were also on that boat along with all of her grandchildren. It turns, ten years later, this elder was now living in the same high-rise apartment building that I was living in. Talk about a small world. One night while we were having a casual conversation about the problems and challenges Somalis have been struggling with since the war, the elder became adamant about not ever going back to Somalia. I was shocked to hear this as most of the elders I've talked to thus far say they just can't wait to get back home and get away from the pressures and alienation so inherent in American culture. Not knowing where the conversation was headed I asked the woman about her family back home. Instantly the tears started welling up in her eyes and running down her weathered cheeks. She began crying as if what had happened ten years ago had just happened only a week ago. She talked about how she was still being haunted by the uncontrollable flashbacks of seeing her daughters and five of her grandchildren floating lifelessly on the sea shore. This tragedy had taken the elders three daughters and thirteen grandchildren away from her. She herself was also on the boat that day and had amazingly survived along with one other grandchild. I say amazing because she had to of been in her early fifties at the time of the accident.

I sure regretted having brought up such an awful memory for her and I tried to comfort her as best I could, but what can anybody really do for a woman who has lost so much. May she and her family be blessed in the afterlife for their tragic loss?

Getting back to 1990, this exodus was becoming more and more draining by the day and at no time prior have I had to use my brain as vigorously as I was during these times. I was constantly questioning my surroundings. Tension kept me prepared for whatever move I may need to make next and one was always extra carful trying not to make the wrong move. We were all challenged beyond our limits and no one was able to hide what they were made of.

Only fourteen years old, but I had a good sense of the dead weight I was trying not to be to this family that had so far helped me escape. So whenever the group had to stop because of staled cars or nightfall, not wanting to be a burden kept me on the look-out for any opportunity to help anyone with anything. One afternoon when we had stopped for a while, I had wondered off looking for some water, a move that would cost me a night without food as I had returned without ever finding any water that night and my host family had already cooked and eaten without me.

My appreciation for this family was being tested. The heartbreak and disappointment set in with my hunger pains. It had always been clear to me how unimportant I was to this family and that created in me a growing sense of resentment towards them.

It took a few long days but we eventually made it to Liboya, Somalia. It was a relatively small town within just a few miles from Kenyan's customs office. Everyone started unloading. The few houses that were in this town were already occupied by its owners so most of us refugees ended up sleeping under trees again. No privacies, no electricity, no clean water and you prayed you wouldn't need a doctor.

There were some wounded militias resting under a tree next to ours. A couple of the men were injured very badly. The man in the most pain was screaming and begging people passing by to finish him. He began expressing his dying regrets for his reactionary decision to fight the rebels. I felt bad for the man and maybe also to satisfy a teenager's curiosity, I went to see if there was anything I could possibly do for him. As I got closer I could see that his stomach organs were hanging out of the side of his body. *"Why did I walk over here to see this"* I thought to myself. The bandages that were put on his wounds were coming loose.

There was nothing I could do for the man and so I continued running, and with quite a different pep in my step. Seeing this mans agony made me feel very fortunate for having made it this far without any physical wounds or limitations. I began to run with a growing sense of optimism in the face of all this death surrounding me.

Later that night I couldn't help but think about what I would have done if that dying man would have been me. Would I have taken my own life? Would I be begging anyone passing by to finish me? I was praying I'd never have to find out.

It was our second day in Liboya. The mother of the family I was with had to call me over so she could lay out all her expectations of me. She made it clear to me what she thought I should be doing if I was planning on riding with her family. She told me I needed to get up early in the morning, go to the water well where everyone was getting their water from and bring some water back to her shelter so they can cook and clean. I was to repeat this routine every morning and in return I would get one meal a day. It sounded like a good deal to me, but I could feel that my welcome was tentative at best.

Those of us who have had to live in a warzone know just how difficult it is to put in words the state of ones mind or the weight that you carry in your stomach all day long. The anguish from witnessing everywhere you look, day in and day out, people lying right where they had been shot in the streets, in their cars or floating down the river. Agony, despair and insecurity haunted us constantly. Trying to maintain some semblance of hope I held on to the conversations with my father who had instilled in me the importance of pursuing an education as a way to secure a brighter future where guns and death were not always at arms length away. Of course getting shot or starving to death seemed a more likely future these days as you couldn't walk a mile without stumbling over bodies or sporadically dodging from the sound of bullets. Yet, through it all I held fast to my dreams of one day going back to school. This dream would give me the motivation I needed to get through this bloody civil war.

As the desire for a higher education and a better life grew deeper in me, I learned to reconcile and accept the fact that my thinking and dreams were far disconnected from the reality that presently existed on the ground. While I'm thinking about books and school everyone else around me is carrying a gun. Young men were attending tribal meetings with elders who were discussing how they will wage war on another tribe. And while these elders and tribal leaders are encouraging these young men to go off and fight, what they are not saying is that these young men are on their own if they get themselves wounded as these so-called leaders are unable to provide any medical attention they may need. Also, none of these leaders are ever going to look out for the wives and children left behind by these young men should they have to pay the ultimate price. I have seen grown men crying, not because they could not accept that their arms or legs were amputated, but because they were no longer able to provide for their loved ones. Seeing all this I decided I would follow my inner convictions telling me that every man has the right to plan his own future and choose his place and the role he believes he should play in the society in which he lives.

By almost any measure, no man deserves to be a refugee. The reality is extremely demeaning for any person to have to live through. I can't imagine how difficult the emotions were for those forced to raise their children under such dire circumstances. Having already dealt with the almost indescribable devastation of Kismayo, I found the life of a refugee beyond frightening and beyond despair. There just are no words to describe the many feelings you encounter as a refugee. I had no money. Most everyone around me was without money. Between the homelessness and having absolutely no idea where our next meal would be coming from, there's just no possible exaggeration of the constant traumas we had to cope with.

Upon reaching the boarder between Kenya and Somalia, I found myself sleeping under different trees night after night. If you were fortunate enough to luck-up on a meal it just about made your whole day as going a day or more without food was the norm. I can only imagine now that it was my youthfulness that gave me the strength to deal with the stress that road me constantly. There were so many moments when I thought I wouldn't be able to take it anymore. I had to start hustling and develop some survival skills quickly.

People were dying everywhere from diseases, starvation, and from untreated gunshot wounds. Death seemed to be the only thing to look forward to around here. It was hard to imagine any other outcome.

While crossing the boarder much of our time was spent sitting around drinking tea and listening to the older guys discussing their predictions about what they thought might happen next as they held fast to their AK 47's and M16's. The smallest disagreements created tensions that kept everyone on edge. One man who we'd come to call Ali, he began suggesting that we had no choice but to go back and face our enemies. I thought about some of the brothers I'd passed who had been left to rot in their regrets for that same line of reactionary thinking.

Ali continued, saying that as we were now at the boarder with nowhere to run, it was our God given right and duty to fight and if need be, die for our properties and our families. He seemed to be getting everyone's attention, and right before he put his next thought in words, we heard a crashing BOOM! Something very powerful had just landed right in the middle of our circle. Everyone instantly hit the ground. We were frozen in silence as hot rocks and dust fell on all of us. Miraculously no one got hurt! We were all completely amazed with what had just taken place right in front of our very eyes. We had an RPG land in front of us and for some unexplainable reason the rocket had not yet exploded. Of course there was no time to even appreciate our fate as we were completely paralyzed by the fear of knowing that this deadly object sitting in front of us might yet go off at any minute. Everybody slowly, slowly crept away!

Manual water wells are used throughout the Somalia countryside. The first couple of days of fetching water didn't seem too bad and we were feeling some relief from having survived thus far. Also our minds were constantly preoccupied with what might happen next. As the days passed and the flow of refugees continued to cluster, it shouldn't be hard to imagine how the usually easy task of pumping water has added to our frustrations now that some thirty thousand people are trying to extract water from a well which previously had only to service the two maybe three hundred peoples who lived on the countryside.

I spent a good two weeks getting up before the sun rose, waiting all day in a long line just hoping I'd get some water before the sun would set that evening. As the weeks passed and more refugees continued to come, the line for water would move so slowly at times it seemed to have come to a complete halt. People would leave some personal item to mark their place in the line, leave for a few hours and then they would come back to their marker that had reserved their place.

Each day I would return to my site where the family that had been aiding my escape was anticipating the water I would be bringing. Each day I would return later and later until eventually, after waiting all day and night in line, I would return two nights in a row without any water which didn't sit well with the elder as she had made loud and clear to me. The pressure made me very uncomfortable. The tentativeness of this relationship was surfacing and I felt like I was being disrespected. I began to doubt myself and I started worrying about all the other unexpected obstacles that were still waiting to be thrown my way.

A part of me wanted to lash out at this family but I knew that they had already done a lot for me. Yet the more we traveled together the more their behavior towards me was becoming annoying and eventually depressing. I knew I was overstaying my welcome and that it was time for me to part from this family. No "Goodbyes", no "Thank you". I woke up one morning and decided to make my own way. Still a teenager, alone in a war zone, starving, determined, and destined to survive this.

Over time I would meet other young brothers who, like me, were without family and for that reason we clicked and began looking out for each other. Although we were far from the gunshots that ran us from our homes, people were still dying all around us. I'll never forget passing a brother who had been propped up on a tree. Apparently someone had used sticks and some cardboard to create some shade for the man who was just lying there suffering from maybe an exploded hand grenade as there were bandages all over his body and he just couldn't move.

Whether it was getting food or just finding a place to stay for the night, I've learned how to hustle and create opportunities for myself. Lacking the basic necessities such as water, food, and shelter as we faced while crossing the boarder, this had fundamentally hampered my journey. It also frustrated my relationships with others. The littlest things would set my temper off. One night I stood up in front of my comrades and suggested that we should go out there and get something to eat. There were four of us boys and one of the other three said, *"How is that going to be possible? We have no money; nor do we have any family here"*. *"Look!"* I said to the boy as I pointed, *"do you see that woman over there cooking white rice on the stove?"* *"Well"*, I continued, *"We are going to robe her after she finishes cooking that rice and this is how it's going to be done! One of us is going to slap her right across her face and another of you will grab the pan and run with whatever is in it"!* One of the boys expressed his fear and saying, *"this is not a good idea, and I don't know if I want be part of it".* I knew that this was some very unusual behavior for us young Somali boys, but I was not about to starve to death. I had to get in this young mans face and say, *"Boy you'd better listen to me, if you don't want to be a part of this mission of feeding the hungry children you will starve alone 'cause I'm eatin' tonight".* In fact, as I look back at these actions now later in my life, I still couldn't agree more. Call that mission 'Feeding the Starving Children", for children we were and we had been starving for days now.

Knowing no other way to come up with some food we all eventually came to an agreement that we had to carry out this unusual rogue mission. We slowly approached the poor unsuspecting black woman and I kindly asked if we could just sit around the fire to warm up for a while. She seemed to have no problem with us. There was no way she could have known what exactly we were up to as we came off as the innocent youths we had been all our lives.

We were very uncomfortable with what we saw ourselves doing but we were so hungry it felt like a life or death choice. We knew that everyday we did not eat made our survival less likely and after going days without food we weren't sure how many more days would pass before we would come across another opportunity to nourish our bodies. Perhaps I'm just trying to justify why we had to slap that woman and run into the dark woods with the meal she had prepared for her own children. I'll never forget that woman whom because of, I slept better than I had in many nights prior. Also that night I would apologize for the inconveniences I knew we had caused that woman's family. I could only hope that she had only missed one meal as me and my comrades had gone many nights without any food.

As soon as the violence reached Liboya, Kenya I was determined to make it to the refugee camps in Mombasa (A.K.A Utanga) no matter how far or what obstacles awaited me. I'd come to far and had seen to much to give up now.

Our greatest fear was the Kenyan police, who were well aware of are plight and are known to ask for money, taking advantage of any Somali refugees traveling without the proper documents. Day after day I would watch people leave in the morning headed for Nairobi only to have returned before sunset because they had been stopped by police officers who they could not afford to keep paying as you could literally run into dozens of officers before you would actually make it to the camp. How a government police force could be so morally corrupt was daunting beyond words. Of course the world knows that Kenya is not the only country facing such challenges, but for African peoples coming from such rich cultures and loving mothers, it's just ridiculous how we treat each other ***throughout*** Africa, the cradle of civilization. And from what I can tell, we Africans should blame no one but ourselves. Having dealt with such difficulties changing the course of our lives we shouldn't expect an outsider to come in and rectify the situation for us.

God has so blessed the Congo with so much in gold and diamonds and yet the children are starving and dying from diseases that have been curable. Nigeria, blessed with so much oil of which nearly 10% is sold to the U.S.A. and yet her citizenry live without electricity and can't even afford to feed their children. I read articles about the Sudanese governments desire to host, in Sudan, negotiations between the T.N.G and the Somalian Islamic Courts. Now what in God's humble name is going on here? If the Somali Islamic Court and the TNG are really serious about peace and reconciliation in Somalia, then why in the world would they go to a government that has been cited for committing genocide on its own people? Is this the model the T.N.G and S.I.C. are looking to, to solve Somalia's problems? Shouldn't the Sudanese government be looking to fix the problems in her back yard?

When there's nothing else to preoccupy your attention all you can do is think too much. I tried anything I could to stop the images that kept repeating in my head but nothing seemed to work. When the only thing around you is sickness, starvation and death, you really have no choice but to try to figure out how you are going to escape this haunting reality. I spent days thinking about how I was going to come up with the 500 shillings I needed in order to pay a smuggler to take me to Mombasa, Kenya. I knew I had no other choice but to leave Somalia as the madness was really getting into my head. The fear of not knowing what might happen next kept me vexed. My main concern at this time was to somehow make some money which in itself was daunting just to think about as there were no jobs.

When this is the case, it's incredibly easy to start doing activities that take you out of your character. Stealing used dishes, clothes or whatever you could find of value was one of the few options that were available. Selling stolen Merchandise was the most accessible way to make money and it was not an easy task by any means. On a good day you may actually luck-up and find some guns.

You had to be smart when conducting business in this way. The timing had to be perfect as you could very simply get your head blown right off your body. Because of these foreseeable risks, I had to develop a set of rules. A majority of my business must be conducted in the day light hours as these villagers are known to have the habit of shooting anything that moves at night. After successfully attaining some merchandise, the product must be carefully sold on the opposite side of town.

During these operations I collected 750 shillings which was more than I needed to get bribe the Kenyan police.

In no way was I proud of earning money in the fashions that I did. However, I must admit, I was damn happy when after it all I was on my way to the Utanga Refugee camp in Mombasa, Kenya.

Finally I would arrive in Mombasa. It was a spectacularly beautiful city. There was an immediate relief in seeing buildings with windows and ceilings still in tact. *"Where is this place?"*, a little voice inside me was asking as we past by the sign that stated '**Welcome to Mombasa, Kenya**'. When we got off the truck and looked around I was completely taken aback seeing people well dressed, smiling and possessing a very relaxed mood that was nothing like the anxiety most of us had been living with for months. In fact their comfort made me aware of myself. I spent a couple of hours just walking around the city. It took maybe an hour or so before I could begin to let go of some of the tension I'd developed from the constant paralyzing sounds of gunshots and death.

Eventually I would find myself on a bus and on my way to the Utunga Refugee Camp which was about a thirty minute ride from the city of Mombasa. As we drove through the well lit, clean and traffic controlled streets, I was bombarded with mixed emotions of admiration, jealousy and resentment. I couldn't get over how Mogadishu had become so dark and scary and I saw nothing about Kenyans that made them any more deserving of such seeming serenity.

At last, the bus arrived at our destination. Since I had no belongings, I got off the bus and just walked around the camp hoping I'd see anyone I knew.

Unlike the Kenyans I saw earlier, those of us at the refugee camp looked exhausted with worry. Our lives had become a complete disaster. There were groups of people sitting together sharing their experiences and pains, asking each other about family member's whereabouts. Others were inquiring of the latest news about the war. I myself had yet to come across a single person I knew and none of these people seemed to even notice the despair and loneliness that haunted me as well. In fact they made me feel like I was some kind of beast. The journey that I was so determined to make was becoming too much for me so full of twists and turns and running into one obstacle after another. Looking back now, I don't know how I handled it all as well as I did being such a young man. As darkness began to set in my longing to see anyone I knew sunk deeper into my stomach. The frustration was unshakable. *"What am I going to do tonight?"* I thought. *"Where am I going to sleep?"* *"Will I ever see my parents or relatives?"* and most importantly *"who's my enemy?"* Seeing an empty shed I decided to sit down and try to put things in perspective. Not 'til the sun woke me up the next morning did I even realize that I had fast fallen asleep. And while I seemed to have escaped the worst part of the violence, there wasn't much relief awakening to another day of hassling, headache and uncertainty over this nightmare that seemed to promise no end.

By this time poverty and hunger had crushed our spirits. Frustration was written all over everybody's face as we were completely helpless. And if being run out of our homeland to live in a refugee camp wasn't bad enough the Kenyan police are now beating us as if we were animals. They'd get us up early in the morning to have us stand in long lines waiting for food from the UN workers. The Kenyan police were walking around beating people up with their sticks in the name of 'keeping us in line' making sure no one cuts in front of someone else, e.t.c. I was absolutely disgusted by what I was seeing. The culture shock was such that Mogadishu didn't even exist any more. Our history, our culture and the art, my dear Somalia, how would she survive such tragic displacement?

We were all aware that much of the world was paying close attention to what was taking place. The images that were being shown on TV sets were so horrible that it caused the first J. W. Bush go visit Mogadishu. So the United States has now sent some 20,000 of its troops into Mogadishu along with troops from Canada, Europe and some troops from Pakistan as well, all who were soon going to face certain death in the streets of Mogadishu. People were collapsing from starvation and many preventable diseases were the causes of many more deaths.

Having had to survive for six months in the jungle was an experience that has taught me how to hustle anything I could. Coming to Kukuyu land with a foreign Somali tongue made awfully difficult the everyday things like buying products or finding a doctor. Having spent some time making friends with the locals I began to learn some Swahili. With a confidence backed by the shear fear of missing any opportunity I would begin to convince my fellow refugees that I could translate Swahili for them.

My first customer was a woman whom I'll call 'Ida'. She wanted to buy supplies for her little kiosk back in the refugee camp and so, I agreed to go with her to Mombasa. We never discussed any money. Among us Somalis there is an "unwritten law" which goes without ever being spoken of. We both knew she would pay me. I just didn't know how much, nor did I care. A few days ago I was dodging bullets on a battlefield where people were getting killed left and right. Can you imagine how excited I felt this morning riding on a bus to Mombasa hired by this woman?

As soon as we got off the bus we came across a shop with candy bars which Ida thought she would be able to sell back at the camp. She asked me to try to negotiate a reasonable price for her. I don't believe she had any idea how nervous I *really* was. The truth was I barely knew any Swahili at all. I kept reminding myself that soldiers don't cry in times of danger and so, with nothing else to loose I began negotiating until I finally talked the shop owner into a deal that Ida was comfortable with buying three boxes of candy bars.

We stopped at two other stores before we finally called it a day. After it all I had made 50 schillings and earned a free a lunch for my services. I was so ecstatic I almost didn't know what to do with myself. On the bus ride home I started thinking about all the other ways I could help refugees and make some money in the process.

Before me and Ida parted that day she promised me that she would tell all her family and friends about my services and sure enough the customers began to flow. Before I knew it I was taking two and three people at a time. On most days' my helping people went pretty smooth but I'll never forget the woman who had a tooth ache and asked me if I could take her to find a dentist. Once we found a dentist she specifically told me that she didn't want the tooth pulled out. Apparently that request had got lost in the translation. I can't tell you the guilt I felt seeing how upset the woman was and if things weren't awkward enough, I still needed to collect for my services. I was relieved by her laughter as she told me *"No, no son, it's not your fault, it's that stupid dentist. He felt the need to remove my tooth in order to make more money!"* Not for one minute did she ever suspect that my translation had anything to do with her tooth being pulled.

Throughout all this, I realized how resilient and creative human beings can be if given a chance. With so much human potential I don't understand why the leaders of my war torn country still struggle to develop an effective and reliable solution for the suffering of my people.

I've never doubted the possibility of my dreams of one day making it to America but even while I was actually sitting on the plane America bound there was still a part of me that couldn't believe it was finally happening. Pinching myself all of the twenty plus hours of the flight and yet my relief was still not complete as I was determined to use my new found opportunity to help those still burdened back home. Of course there were plenty of challenges waiting for me, but just as hope got me through some six months of living in the jungles of Somalia, I suddenly found myself rejuvenated by the odds I've already overcome. How can I give up now? I knew I'd face language barriers when I got to America. I knew there would be some culture shock upon my arrival. And of course I had to fight off the haunting fears of competing in an infrastructure the size of which I've never experienced. Yet all these worries paled when compared to my confidence. With a heart full of mixed emotions; loss, amazement and exploding ambitions, all I could do was picture my skinny ass walking through the concrete jungles of the Americas I grew up seeing in magazines and movies throughout my youth. *"Don't worry momma, I'm alright and I'll be back for ya' soon!"*

Wow, Washington DC. I've never seen anything like this place that was bigger than anything I could have ever imagined. The buildings and roads, traffic lights, paved sidewalks, Stores, malls and shopping centers. Coming from Somalia one can easily be overwhelmed by the sheer magnitude of the architectural infrastructure. I felt like I could have just stood on the corner all day long watching all the cars and people pass by. Everyone seemed to be generally happy. I couldn't help but wonder what their lives were like. I knew they ate plenty as I've never seen so many fat people. *"No one looks like they've ever gone a day without food"* I thought seeing all of the overweight people. Everyone seemed to have nice houses, nice cars and good paying jobs and seeing family members together reminded me of the emptiness I felt being in a strange land with no family myself.

After about a year and some months I had been able to pick up quite a few English words and I was also starting to make friends. Me and my cousins starting hanging around our new found American friends. You know, doing things we were seeing other youths doing, going to malls, going to clubs at night or just killing time passing blunts around. My cousin seemed to like this lifestyle a little more than I did. But throughout all that 'Partying like a Rock Star' I started getting to know girls which, is an important part of any cultural transition.

We had both found jobs fairly quickly. I found a job working at a grocery store in Arlington, VA, stacking frozen and non frozen foods in the back of the store. Around the first two weeks of the month I would have to work the cash register. I grew to dread working as a cashier as this job required interacting with customers who were not always so nice. They often seemed pushy and they were almost always in a hurry. Many were so taken by my presence that they'd get agitated and begin fumbling unnecessarily. There attitudes created pressures I've almost never known and I was still trying to better my English. How I grew to regret having to ask a customer to please repeat themselves. This alone was enough for many people to get an attitude which did not make anything easier for either of us. Often a person might have some four or five items that wouldn't scan or maybe the product might not have had a price on it. For these situations there was a five page list next to the register where you could look up the right price. Well, this would be helpful if you knew the name of the product you were looking for. I remember the pressures mounting as my grocery lines were getting longer and longer. My manager was constantly getting pissed off because she would always have to stop what she was doing so she could come over and help me find a price for an item or open another register.

My manager was an elder black lady. She had to of been in her mid to late fifties. She was a really nice lady and a woman of few words. In fact I can't remember her having much of a conversation with anyone.

Nevertheless she was very nice to me and I really came to appreciate that she never talked to me longer than she usually did. It was hard for me to comprehend a lot of what she was trying to tell me and she was sensitive to my barriers which made it much easier for me. I worked for that woman for almost a whole year. There would be times when I would get called to the front and be asked to go in the back storage area to find a product I couldn't even name. I'd be wondering around seemingly thousands of foreign products for a couple minutes before I would give up and find a place to hide until I'd eventually hear the manager coming, "*Where is that god damn,* or "*where in the hell is that mother f------ African boy?*", I would hear her mumbling these things as she was looking for the product. Then she continue cussing me out as she left to tend to the waiting customer. After dealing with the customer she would come up with some way to punish me. She grew quite used to clenching her fist and hitting me in the back of the head whenever I would bring her the wrong product. Of course there were a few times when I felt like reminding her that she'd been speaking the language for almost sixty years, but usually she didn't bothered me one bit. I used to say to myself "*hit me all you feel is necessary mamma; just don't show me the door*".

Out one afternoon walking around the city of Arlington, VA, I was looking for a job when I passed by a gas station and noticed how busy the place was. There was a Korean woman working at the cash register and she was moving as fast as she could just to try to keep pace with the constant flow of people. Her frustration was written all over her face as she was no match for all the customers she had coming and going. It was obvious she needed some help as she seemed to be the only person working in the store as far as I could tell. "*How could they turn me down*" I thought, so, I walked casually in the store, grabbed some pop and chips and got in line. I had intended on asking the cashier about a job but by the time she got to me four more people had already gotten behind me. It seemed like a bad time to interrupt her so I decided to come back the next day when I would hopefully catch the manager at a less busy time.

The next morning I got up bright and earlier and headed out on my four mile walk to my new found opportunity. As it turned out, the woman who was working the cashier was actually the store manager. After introducing myself I asked if they could use some help. The cashier went to the back of the store and came right back out with her sister who was the owner of the place. They seemed to have received me well and within a few days I was working again.

I spent the first two weeks training with these women during the morning shift before they would eventually move me to the second shift where I would finally meet my night co-worker John. I'd seen him coming to work when my shift ended and I grew curious about the old man. He was an elder white man and I was wondering what unfortunate circumstances had him working nights at a gas station and in a neighborhood as ruff as this one. He seemed an alright person at first until he started whining about having worked so hard all his life competing with minorities for jobs. And if that wasn't odd enough he would later tell me that he was taking female hormone shots to help ease the pain from the cancer growing in his groin. With a smile on his face the man went on about how he was only able to use his tongue to please his woman. We laughed together but I couldn't believe he was revealing so much personal stuff to a complete stranger and the best was yet to come. Before I knew it john started talking about black and Hispanic peoples like I wasn't one of them. *"Nigger this, Niger that"*. It was coming out his mouth all night long. *"I wish they'd all just get on a big boat and go back to wherever in the hell they came from"* he'd say unscrupulously. I was so shocked I didn't even know how to respond. I had certainly heard much about racism in America but I was under the impression that it was an age old thing. This was my first face-to-face encounter with an actual bigot and he continued on even asking me if I knew where black people had come from? *"There from AFRICA"* I snarled *"the same place I'm from!* I was trying to give him a hint that his comments were very much putting me on edge. Of course he didn't seem to be getting the point. *"No, No"* he started *"A Native American was having sex with a buffalo and it became pregnant with a black baby, that's were them assholes came from".* I thought that that was more than I would be able to take. When my shift was over I went home and the only thing I could think about all night long was what I was going to do to this idiot fucking white man. I was having thoughts about getting a beer bottle and ending his misery but I calmed myself as I started thinking about how important my success was to my country. Seeing the big picture, I knew I had to control my anger. And while I had a green card I knew I had to avoid fighting and stay out of any trouble as it may be used against me when it came for my citizenship. So, all I could do was ignore this pitifully miserable old man who I ended up working with for the next three years. Ironically we ended up becoming good friends as he could only appreciate all the physical work around the shop that I kept him from having to do. I kept him from having to mop the floors, which was his duty, I rang the customers up fast and I was always going outside and helping customers with the gas pumps when they needed it. One night he had gotten beat-up walking home from work so I started giving him a ride home to his apartment after work.

After some time John began to change his attitude, towards me anyway. In fact, one night he would try to recant some of his earlier comments to me saying that *"I really don't have any problems with black people from Africa and I like you and your friend from Sierra Leon, it's those damn nigger Americans I can't stand"*. I knew the man had no idea how his comments made me feel so I took the high road and continued to do whatever I could to help him. What the hell, the man was sixty years old, he had a difficult life growing up and he was sick. Sure he was blaming the wrong people for his problems but what was I going to do? Of course there were times that he was as pleasant to the stores black customers as he was always to the white patrons. I had to ask him about this. He would tell me that when the pain in his groin was acting up he would loose his patience easily with people. So, for three years I put up with the old man and for three years I would go home and tell my friends all the crazy things the man would say. My friends couldn't understand how I was able to put up with some of the very extreme comments Robert would make. They would tell me I should of said this or did that and that I should be looking for another job, but I just kept my eye on the prize and wasn't about to let some old fool keep me from it. John had been working at this store for some 11/12 years so the whole neighborhood knew about the ranting old man, but he was certainly no threat to anybody, certainly not me.

Robert was a church going man and on Wednesdays he would always bring me some food from the church socials he'd attended. I would thank him, take the food to the back office and throw that shit right in the trash. Are you kidding me? There was no way I was going to put anything in my mouth that came from this racist cracker. I have no problem accepting food from a church but even the old women who would come to the job to speak with him from time to time; they seemed to have the same demeanor as did old Robert.

Working two jobs and being able to go home to an apartment and a nice warm bed, this was a beautiful thing to me. I was infatuated with what to me seemed to be quit a fortune that I've found here in Arlington, VA. I loved getting paid every Friday. I loved being able to pay my bills, spending some money and sending some money home as well. However, it didn't take long for the economic situation to become clear and soon I would no longer be satisfied. I was becoming aware of a growing emptiness inside of me. I started feeling like I was letting myself down as well as those I've left behind. I had to stop and ask myself *"what is happening to me?"* The drugs and partying definitely was not me and I knew I would never reach my goals if I went that rout. I wasn't even in school which was what fed my motivation and optimism in the first place. I have always believed that education was the best way to avoid a life of poverty that has unfortunately plagued billions of Africans, especially. Trying to walk the straight and narrow, I was living a very meager lifestyle collecting two pay checks every Friday from two different employers and I was still barely paying my bills. My cousin on the other hand, he had quit his job and has been spending nothing but twenties and hundreds ever since. It was humbling always having to go back to him for money that he was growing tired of borrowing me. And while I was slaving for much of nothing spending most of my time working, my baby cousin was becoming quit well known in the neighborhood. He seemed to be making all kinds of friends. He had people hanging around him all the time - mainly because he was taking care of them. He was picking up their drink tabs at bars and taking them to restaurants, just buying all kinds of friends that I couldn't make for years. I mean, my little cousin had people coming up and asking me if I knew 'Bulldog'. I had no idea the streets had given' my cousin a name. I was shocked the first time I saw him respond to someone calling him Bulldog.

He seemed to be on top of his game courting fly young women and having people laughing at every other word he said. He was always the center of attention and he always had people driving him around, shopping everyday. This was not the kid I knew. In fact he moved from where we were living and rented himself a one bedroom apartment downtown. When visiting him I was shocked to find his apartment was cluttered with clothes (mostly women's), dirty dishes and fast food boxes everywhere. I was taken aback by the whole scene. Part of me began saying *"Man, I need to get my hustle on!"* I spent the next few days fantasizing about all the things I could do with the hundreds of dollars I'd have if only I would take the risks bulldog seemed to have no problems with.

Looking back now, seeing all the trouble this fast life has brought him, the prison sentences and all the difficulties that come from having been locked up, I've since learned to appreciate the narrow path I chose.

Soccer (called football in most parts of the world) was the main sport played in Somalia and just like every one of my peers I grew up playing religiously with the dream of some day becoming a great world famous soccer player. When I left Africa I had no idea that I'd never again play the sport I grew up loving. Nor did I know how much more I would grow to love the game of Basketball? I would play the game late into the evening and when I wasn't playing I was looking for a game on T.V. Michael Jordan, Patrick Ewing and Sean Kemp were the names I had come to know as these brother's personalities and their ball game fascinated me. I found the game to be a great escape and release while I was earning my Electrical/ Electronics Degree.

There were many things that drew me to the field of electronics. I used to visualize myself working as an electronics technician repairing things. I was living near the Northern Virginia Community Collage and it was fairly inexpensive so, I enrolled in their English, math, history and social studies classes. Because it was a community collage I was required to take these general classes before I could study electronics.

I was only working one job at the time which wasn't cutting it. I ended up dropping out of the collage twice during that first two years and had only completed two semesters each of the two years that I attended. Again I found myself frustrated at the stagnation towards my educational goals. I felt like my life was not going anywhere and while I didn't want to admit it to myself, I was beginning to give up.

While attending this community collage I would meet a beautiful, dark skinned sister named Cumbaro. I was very attracted to her. We started out having short casual conversations and before you know it we were hanging out together all the time eating at different Chinese restaurants and we both loved Kentucky Fried Chicken. My feelings for this sister were growing deeper as not a day would go by that we didn't spend some time together. Of course my friends knew about us and she had told a few of her girlfriends but she wanted to keep our relationship as private as possible which I had no problem with. The relationship lasted for a good year and a half which made it hard to hide from her family. As we fell deeper in love we had started talking about marriage and children. I was really taken by this girl. Of course we were young and as the family got involved immaturity and anger got the best of us and we started to drift apart. She had taken a trip back to Africa for a couple of months in which time I had decided to move to MPLS, MN and would never see my girl, Cumbaro again.

After six years of living and working in Arlington, VA I was growing frustrated by my fruitless attempts at achieving the collage degree I so passionately desired. It was time to make some different moves, so, I called a friend of mine who was living in Minneapolis, MN and asked him what life was like up north. I asked him how reasonable the renter's situation was and if the jobs were plenty and paying? *"This place is perfect for you"* he told me. On and on he went talking about how amazing Minneapolis was. He had gotten me pretty excited, especially when he began to relay all he'd learned about the many collages that would be available to me. He had long known of my desire to go collage and he had identified with my frustration with the pace of things. Of course it was equally important that I find viable work while I go to school as there were a large number of people back in Somalia that were still very dependent on what I was able to send them. There was no way I could turn my back on them.

Always one up for new experiences it didn't take much to convince me to move to Minnesota. Although I knew Bulldog would not be so anxious to leave as he seemed to have grown pretty comfortable with his ghetto lifestyle image. I couldn't imagine how compelling it really was considering he'd already been bed ridden for two months when a couple of thugs had broken his legs and he'd had a gun pulled on him on many an occasion. Bulldog himself never owned or carried a gun although he projected the kind of persona that would make you think he had one. At six foot 300 lbs coming from a place as friendly as Africa bulldog never possessed the kind of fear that would make him think he would need a gun and he wasn't the kind of person who would shoot somebody over money or drugs. As hard as he played I knew he had to of had some fear of where this lifestyle could possible lead but you know how it is when your young and feeling invincible, you never expect anything to go wrong. After discussing the options with Bulldog I guess he had been robed enough to realize it wasn't such a bad idea to leave and start over somewhere else. We would eventually pack-up our few belongings and before we knew it we were on a greyhound bus heading up north, leaving behind the Virginia 'Two-step' only thinking forward about the new opportunities we would be creating for ourselves somewhere else. With an Associates Degree in mind I was planning on visiting each and every private collage I could. With my renewed determination, I vowed that this time nothing was going to come between me and my goals.

The bus ride from Washington D.C. to Minneapolis, MN was a good four day ride which made for plenty of time to try to have some good sense conversation with my cousin about his new found pimp and drug dealing, wanna-be hardcore gangster ways. I couldn't get over how much he had changed since we've come to America and I was worried that he was going to play the role right to the penitentiary or worse, the grave, a side of this gangster reality these actors and models on television were not too often showing. Having been exposed to Tupac, Biggie Smalls and J-Z, now, like so many other Africans finding themselves often in dire financial situations they hadn't anticipated and before they ever saw it coming, they've fallen right into the traps to which the puppeteers mirages have lead them and often times when there were worlds of other things we could otherwise have been doing. My cousin was like many Africans aspiring to come to America seduced by the lore of magazines and movies that made it seem like people in America were living the lifestyles of a Whitney Houston and a Bobby Brown. You can't see the pressures it takes to hold up the facades you see in a magazine add, nor can you see the everyday life pressures going on behind the scenes of a movie setting. In America the Image of the black is so sophisticatedly demonized that young impressionable Africans are adopting all kinds of symbolic and destructive behaviors, postures and exotic expensive clothing and lifestyles just trying to assimilate.

Prisons are one of America's most lucrative businesses and the systematic genocide of black people feeds the insatiable beast. I was trying to get my cousin to reflect on these things about this America that he seems to have taken so completely for granted. I was trying to inspire him to think of this move as a new start, leaving behind that which comes as easy as does the problems and troubles it entails. My cousin had changed so much since we've moved to America I swear at times I felt like I didn't know him at all. We both wanted a better life for ourselves but we were considering quite different means for reaching considerably different ends. It was becoming more and more obvious to me that we were becoming two entirely different people. Of course we were still family and I wanted to help him see other possibilities other than those myths perpetuate about black men being gangsters. Considering the risks he'd taken and the close calls, his life of instant gratification didn't seem to be doing him as well as he'd like to think. For the most part I respected his entrepreneurial ship. Hell, he was making money hand over fist twenty-four/seven. At times I was downright envious and there seemed to never be a dull moment with this guy. He had woman selling their bodies for him and men selling his drugs. He was never a real big time hustler but he was no joke either hustling ghetto people where ever we went and whenever he had a chance. Even I was doing errands for him from time to time picking people up and dropping them off because bulldog had had his license revoked, so, whenever he needed me to go get someone he'd just hand me a stack of money with a rubber band tied around it, give me a name and some directions and off I would go. I don't think he ever knew how much money was in the stacks he had given me. If I found myself needing some money I'd call him up and cuss him out for only having given me maybe three hundred dollars. He'd apologize and give me some more money like it was nothing to him. My cousin kept on moving for that money but he had not a greedy bone in his body when it came to taking care of those around him and I knew it wasn't going to be easy for him to just get up and walk away from the reputation and lifestyle he'd established for himself. And while I had talked him into moving to Minneapolis with me, something told me that hoping he'd change his lifestyle was wishful thinking, but I couldn't give up on him. Anyways, his lifestyle made for a stepping stone many a time and was now making for a comfortable transition to Minnesota. He paid six months worth of rent and groceries most of which was still fast food.

During the bus ride I tried to talk seriously to Bulldog asking him what he thought he would do once we got to Minneapolis. *"You know me, dog, I'm hustler"* he said. *Come-on cousin"* I said *"can't you be serious for just once in your life and speak like the grown intelligent man we both know you are? This is s chance for you to give all that bullshit a clean break"* I continued *"why don't you start thinking about going to school and finding a job for some respectable income".* He just grinned at me as he usually does right before he starts with the fast talking he swears he's so good at, *"alright man, here's the plan; You know I got a little bit of money for us okay. I need you to hold the money so you can go get us an apartment, then you can go ahead and find a job or go to school or something. I'm just going to relax for two months and try to clear my head man, you know, all that marijuana and vodka and shit I've been doing for so long now, damn, I just need some time get it all out of my system dog".* I guess! Bulldogs got his plans and I got mines. Within two weeks I was able to find job and I had gathered information from three different collages all within the Twin Cities. Within eight months I was enrolled at Northern Electronic Institute (N.E.I college of technology) one of the best private collages in the Midwest. I'll never forget the day I walked into the admissions office. *"Hello!, I am Alice"* the lady behind the desk said politely. We talked for a few minutes and she seemed to of received me well and responded positively to my excitement. I filled out some paperwork, took a few tests and prayed for the admission papers to arrive in my mailbox, which it eventually did. I'll never forget how good I felt riding on the bus on the way to school that first morning as my mind was racing as I was thinking about all the different things I was going to be able to do once I got that magic paper in my hand. Classes started at 7 am and went all day until 2 o' clock that afternoon and five days a week. There were about thirty people in the class. Only two of us were black and we seemed to both of been glad to see each other. One of the two female students in the class was Asian.

I made it through the first semester with no problems passing all my classes and even made some friends. Me and my new friends had enrolled in a three-on-three basketball tournament that we had practiced for during our lunch hours and after school as well. Things were going just great as I was counting down the semesters "*four to go*" It wasn't until about the third quarter when working full time was again wearing me down. I was quite familiar with this downward spiral as I'd been down it before but this time I decided that I was going to stop working and stay in school as I was determined to graduate. Continuing with my morning classes and staying late afterschool hanging out with my study group, I would have my homework done before I even went home. I wasn't doing so bad for the first month of being unemployed but by the middle of the second month I was so broke, without a car or even money for a bus pass, I was getting up before sunrise and walking downtown where there were usually a lot more people getting on and off busses. I'd be their early in the morning just hoping to catch someone getting off a bus and throwing their bus transfer away. Of course once I got to school I had no problem coming up with a ride home but those early cold Minnesota winter mornings made for some challenges staying in school. I could have asked any of my new friends to pick me up in the mornings and they'd of done it no problem I'm sure, but I didn't want any of them to worry about my temporary predicament. Besides, considering people back home had no even regular clean water to drink I was to busy focused on the opportunities I had and couldn't see any permanent obstacles. I was going to have my degree just as I'd been envisioning.

While the obstacles and challenges continued to mount I drew strength from the growing excitement of knowing that my graduation ceremony was just six short months from now. I was so determined to complete the course that to keep from dropping out of school again, as capitalism had forced me to twice already back when I was living in Virginia; so to avoid repeating my past failures, I ended up taking on a job working the graveyard shift for a grocery store. Never could I have imagined how difficult this routine would become. When I got off of work in the morning I would go straight to school. I've never been a breakfast eater and living in the jungle taught me to be content on less so I could deal with not eating too much. And while I could deal with a little hunger, fatigue was something I wasn't so prepared for. I was so tired by the middle of the school/work week that I often found myself falling asleep in the different classes thru-out the school day. Mind you, I'm in school studying 'Electronics'. All day we are building circuits, soldering and stripping wires, these practices require ones full focus for safety reasons of course.

My boss was so glad that she had someone stocking foodstuffs during those ridiculous hours. I just let her go-on believing I loved the job even though I knew it was at best a temporary situation as sleep deprivation would drive anybody crazy. I remember getting off of work in the mornings after having been up working on my feet all night long. There's no sitting in a grocery store. I'd be so exhausted that at times it was down right painful to stay awake. And when it did get so bad that I wanted to just go home and go to sleep as it was so easy to do; at these times I would think about the millions of young Africans back home who would do anything to be in my shoes. Before I knew it I be counting the months and days left as I had no intentions of breaking my routine until I had that degree in hand.

One morning during class we were soldering components on a circuit board when before I knew it I had fallen asleep and unconsciously grabbed the hot end of a soldering iron. Having burned my palm and all of the five fingers on my right hand I awoke to the smell of my burning flesh. Of course the pain was excruciating, but I just sat their emotionless as my classmates came rushing over to see my hand, a sight that caused most of them to turn away feeling bad for me. Some of the students would tell me that they were shocked at how calm I handled the whole situation. I never brought my personal problems to school so none of my peers had any idea that I was working the crazy hours that I was. After bandaging my burning hand I would go home and straight to sleep. Graveyard shift never got another thought, but of course I was back in school the next day. Coming from the poorest country in the world, on the poorest continent in the world I knew I could handle poverty a little longer. As for my injury, it almost seemed fortunate considering the suffering my eyes have seen. I wasn't bothered at all. I was still on glee thinking about all the opportunities and doors that would be open to me once I got that paper in hand.

It was a sweet September, 2002 at long last I would graduate from NEI, College Of Technology in Columbia Heights, Minnesota, with a Degree in Electronics. When at the graduation ceremony, while the school principal was calling our names as we came on stage to receive our certificate and congrats, I remember regretting not knowing the words to express how absolutely ecstatic I was that night. While for many of my school peers collage was almost an extra curricular activity and often taken for granted, I had been dreaming of and working for this accomplishment for almost as long as I could remember. Having had to drop out of collage twice, having known other kids that have had to drop out because of obstacles that came up in their lives, considering all the maneuvering and sacrifices I've had to make in order to maintain my focus on my goal. I could have quit behind every obstacle; no money, racism and the language barrier was an hourly challenge. I could see how these and other factors could discourage people and cause them to quit but I held on.

The relief from seeing my persistence pay off, it was serene. Some of my classmates invited me to go out and celebrate with them but I just wanted to go home where I could be by myself so as to reflect on it all. A few years ago I was in a jungle running from a war zone conning and stealing from people to keep from starving to death, today I am in arguably the greatest and richest country in the world having earned a collage degree with which I can get a job that pays much more than I'd get flipping burgers at a fast food joint or any of the other jobs I've humbled myself and stuck to in order to reach my goals and I can tell you, looking back it was well worth the sacrifice now having worked for very respectable companies like Fargo Electronics, Gannett offset, which is a major printing shop producing magazines such as U.S.A. Today, City Pages, e.t.c. Presently I am working for Professional Car Wash System's, where I am a Field Service Technician repairing in bay automatic car washes all over the state of Minnesota. I am basically my own boss. Man, can you imagine how good I am feeling these days.

Though I've worked at some very different and interesting places after graduating from college where I've gained a tremendous amount of knowledge, I was in no way prepared for the rewards or challenges that would follow from my next job endeavor.

I was working for Fargo Electronics when, during one of my 15 minute breaks, I came across an advertisement for a job opening at Gannett Off-set, a national printing company. I liked working for the people at Fargo electric and I was making more money than I had ever before, but I knew that with my degree I was eligible for much better pay, so I always kept an ear to the ground so as to not miss better opportunities.

I showed up at the Human resources office at Gannet for an interview that they had scheduled for me. I was expecting to talk to a manager about the job. I was taken completely by surprise when the secretary at the desk handed me a test. *"What the hell"* I thought, I've never heard of having to take a test before ever even talking to someone about the job. I remember trying to hide my surprise as the secretary explained the test to me. I took my time with what consisted of only twelve questions. When I was done I politely handed the test back to the woman hoping she would take it easy on a brother. She then reached under her desk, pulled out an answer key and started correcting my work right on the spot. The next thing I know she was on the phone with the department manager all excited talking about *"Hey, he got 11 out of twelve answers right!"* as she glanced at me with a smile that soothed any remaining worries I had. I knew I did well on the test but I never expected to be the first person to ever get 11 out of 12 questions right. As soon as she hung up the phone the manager came right out to greet me. His name was Randy. He took me on a tour of the plant while he explained to me that Gannet Offset was the sole printing shop for magazines such as 'USA Today', along with other local commercial and neighborhood newspapers.

The Place was huge. They had printing presses, folders and stackers as well as other small but equally important equipment that needed to be maintained. After the tour Randy escorted me back into his office where he continued to ask me a few more routine questions. He also wanted to know my views about my degree.

I felt really good about my interview with Randy. He told me that he would be interviewing other candidates over the next couple of days and he assured me that he would be making a decision within those few days. As he handed me his business card he reminded me to call him back if I hadn't heard from them in two days.

Within the next Twenty four hours, Sue, the secretary from the Human Resources office at Gannet, she would call and congratulate me on being the one they've selected for the position. Can you imagine how they made my day? Almost seeming more pleased than I was; Sue carried on as if she just couldn't wait to tell me all about the job. She told me all about the hourly pay and all the benefits I would be making. Then she asked me if would like to work for them. Without missing a beat I assured her that my enthusiasm at least matched hers although *I* knew where I was coming from. In fact, I knew I was going to take the job as soon as she mentioned what they were paying as I had never gotten paid as much money as they were offering me. Before our phone conversation came to a close, Sue would set up a time for me to go and take both a physical and a drug test, which, of course, I had no issues with. We said our 'See you latter's' and before I hung up the phone I was multiplying my hours by my hourly wage, calculating my newly found daily, weekly, monthly and yearly income.

I spent the first week training with another tech who schooled me on our day to day business. Within a very short amount of time I was doing all the things they needed me to and Randy had noticed how quickly I was catching on. Being the nice guy he was he took me under his wing and showed me everything; he really seemed to appreciate my work ethic and was willing to assist me with whatever my needs were.

I was working in the maintenance department which consisted of 5 other techs, although the company must have been employing some two maybe three thousand people. There were so many people working for this company. Of the five guys I worked with in the maintenance department the only black person was me. In fact I can probably count on one hand how many black people I saw working anywhere in the company. Also I was an immigrant and a Muslim which for some just made for two more strikes against me. Of course being an Immigrant from Africa I've found that the employers are often more comfortable working with Africans from the continent while those same white institutions are usually suspect when it comes to hiring and working with Black Americans.

Well, while the employers are finding much to appreciate within the Africans persona, it was with my fellow employees, my peers if you will, and with many of the older whites I've ran into and had to work with at different jobs and now here at Gannett. These white folks sometimes seem to almost be possessed with a fear and angst of which black skin and the Noun 'Muslim' seems to evoke.

xThe boss had mentioned to me that I had exceeded their expectations. Also, he wrote me up a very good review for me. Usually people had to of been employed for at least a year before they can start working the weekend rotation, but I was doing so well for Gannett that within six months I was doing weekend rotations all by myself which was really a lot of responsibility for a new tech fresh out of school as I was.

I was really pleased with the way things were going but from time to time I would come across a problem that would have me scratching my head and looking for Randy, he was great whenever there was a mechanical problem I couldn't quite figure out. In fact I would often refer to him as my big brother. I just can't thank him enough for all that he's taught and done for me.

So, while I was still very much on glee over my new job, I would be dishonest if I didn't mention how the racism I was experiencing was creating some peculiar atmospheres at the job. You know what they say about 'racism'... easy to see, hard to prove, impossible to deny.

There was this white guy who was working in the same department that I was working in. In fact we shared the same office space. I knew something was wrong with this guy from the get-go. It was the way he was always trying to ignore me which, in itself didn't bother me as he was just one of those old miserable greasy nasty fat fucks from hell. Whenever I'd be returning to the office after some errand I've just had to take care of, I'd catch this bastard whispering to another employee and as soon as we made eye contact they'd start laughing and walk away, making sure to let me know I was the unwelcomed butt of their sarcasm.

I was as offended as anyone would be but I wasn't about to let his nor anybody else's ignorant behavior interfere with my destiny. I knew I had a good job and I wanted to continue working there for at least a good year or as long as possible so as to build my resume and gain all the experience I could. Besides, the old fart was just jealous seeing a young black man making the same money that he was making. In fact I think he was just trying to provoke me so he could have *me* fired for being the trouble maker. So, the retarded cracker continued on with his childish schoolyard antics for almost 8 months and never did I even once complain to my bosses about the matter. In fact I was trying to keep it from my bosses as I expected that they would have fire me before they would even think to fire this Nazi bastard. Unlike this buster I was a mature black man who knew how to co-exist with the white folks even when they weren't always themselves civilized, I knew not to stoop to their level. This guy was a complete nobody as far as I was concerned.

About a year and half had gone by before the bosses eventually did exactly what I had all this time, been trying to avoid. One day the Human Resource's manager, who was a 'friendly?' woman anyway, she had gotten together with my boss Randy and they called me into the office. They began asking me about what had been going on between me and this jerk in particular. Apparently they had been watching the situation for almost six months because, through their other employees, the bosses had been hearing rumors about this white mans sentiments towards me. They told me that they appreciated how well I was handling the situation and they also noted that I didn't seem to be having any problems with anyone else in my department and throughout the facility for that matter. Of course they may not all have liked me as some 90% of the employees where white, but, as my bosses also pointed out, I hadn't had one quarrel with anybody at the company throughout the whole two years that I'd been there. It was obvious to everyone at the company, who, in fact was, the real ass.

Well, since someone had finally asked, I decided that this should be a safe time to open up to these people and say everything that I had been holding inside of me for the last 15 months or so. Honestly speaking, how ever in the world could I have expected them or anyone to do anything about this guy's attitude towards the people that made his journey out of barbarism even possible whether or not he recognizes the gift black people have brought to this world? He wouldn't be the first white person to think that war was a greater contribution to civilization than language, math or man and women's spirituality.

Anyways, I'm sure that one out of these two bosses had the authority to fire and hire whom they pleased, but who would ever think a white man would be fired for his racist behavior let alone for his deformed sentiments towards anybody black? I certainly wasn't the fool.

Back in Somalia many of the people I knew believed that racism in America was something of the past. Now, after having lived in this country for some 16 plus years I see that racism remains... easy to see, hard to prove, impossible to deny. Perhaps that is why I've never complained to anybody whenever I was confronted with it, choosing instead to just put up with it. No one expects racism to just disappear in a thin air , not for any god, not for any mothers and certainly not for some immigrating Somalian cashing in on American dream.

The human resources manager told me that she was going to talk to the guy. *"Yeah right, talk to him? I thought, "About what, Baseball? Hell, this man must be in his late fifties which means he has spent his whole life enjoying all the privileges and benefits that came with being white, and she thinks I am naive enough to think that some "talking to him" is going to do anybody any good? I couldn't believe we were actually having such an illiterate conversation.* "*Listen*" I started as I began rubbing the skin on my hand for them "*This aint Michael Jackson, my skin is always going to be black just like that man is always going to be a racist, which is why in fact, lately, I've been looking for another job.*" They sure didn't like hearing that! "*No, No, Please*" She says" *we really like you hear and we want you to be happy.*" I really hadn't been looking for a job but since everything was now out in the open I actually did start looking for a different company to work for. In the meantime I remained a loyal and enthusiastic employee at Gannet and like I expected, absolutely nothing changed. I could of gotten an attitude and quit but I knew that was exactly what that cracker wanted me to do. Besides, Gannett was paying for some customized training that I was taking at Anoka Technical College and I made enough money in that two years working for this company that I was able to take care of all kinds of short term goals. If I'd a gotten upset and acted a fool I would not accomplished all that I had in that two years. Ignoring the heathens and putting up with the bullshit, it turned out to be worth it if you ask me. And by the way, after six months had gone by since my conversation with the managers, I eventually found a better paying job where I was basically my own boss.

I left Gannett Offset because I found a great paying job fixing car wash machines for Professional Car Wash Systems (P.C.S). They service in bay automatic car washes. These are the car washes where you drive in and the water shoots up from the ground until the sign 'Drive Forward' lights up. It's a very cool mechanical operation. It's got electrical, mechanical and Programmable logic controls, which is what fascinated and drew me to the field of electronic in the first place. The description in the newspaper was saying that this job involves lots of travelling throughout the state of MN and North Dakota. In the seven years that I've lived in state of Minnestoa the only two cities that

I have been to were Minneapolis and The City of St. Paul, I figured *"what better way to discover more about the 'Land of Ten Thousand Lakes', and at someone else's expense?, How could I go wrong?* As I drove to these different towns I began to notice that these small town's people were very different from the people in the city. The further out I drove the more the differences began to stand out. I saw people out here riding horses and pulling carts with kids in them. The scene had me thinking about the whereabouts of my passport and checking my map to make sure I haven't crossed some border into Mexico or someplace. I remember passing by a certain group of people who seemed to have a dress code that distinguished the men from the women. They wore all black outfits with white shirts and all the women wore skirts. I would later learn that these are Amish. And, they are American. Even their children's attire distinguished the boys from the girls. That isn't always the case in the city and if you saw a horse in the city you would be looking around for the rest of the parade.

Since working for P.C.S, I've made friends with store owners, managers and regular employees from towns as remote as a Sleepy Eye, Winona and Gaylord MN all the way to Bismarck and Williston, ND. Those white folks would be sitting around the store just waiting for me to show up and fix their money maker, the town car wash. Unlike some of the bigots I've had to put up with, I could appreciate many of the people I met in these small towns seemed to really appreciate me and I enjoyed the challenges from all the trouble shooting that was involved with my work day.

These small town's people were very different from the people back in the city. Their manners were different as well and they were always eager to start up conversations with me about my culture or maybe different business ventures we could possibly pursue. I've even had one couple tell me that I looked just like their son (obviously an adopted orphan) and they seemed to be trying to let me know that I need not worry about them when the sun goes down.

As much as I appreciated all I've learned from the different jobs I've held since graduating from collage, and as much as I can appreciate working for P.C.S. These guys were making all the big money while I was doing all the work, so, it didn't take long before I started realizing and fantasizing about one day owning my own business. I've met and watched so many Business owners that I'm starting to understand how money changes hands, profit and loss calculation, all these things that we do in our daily lives anyway. Now that I can comfortably troubleshoot, diagnose and repair so many different types of machines and have had good relationships with customers, I started thinking I should really consider owning my own business. I got on the internet and began researching distributers who would sell me spare parts, the chemicals needed, e.t.c Mind you, I was still working for P.C.S. so I had to keep my intentions on the low as I didn't want the company to think I was undermining them.

The busiest time of the year for car -wash companies of course is during the winter season, because people don't want the salt from the streets to rust their vehicles out, so car wash owner's ended up making enough money to offset the slow season.

I had opened my own business just one month before the winter season, so I ended up making quite a bit of money. In fact, I just couldn't believe how much money I actually made within those first five winter months. Springtime being the slow season I found myself without anything to do so; I packed my bags and hopped on an eighteen hour plane ride to Thailand and then China.

It was an eighteen hour plane ride of which I spent most of the time just thinking about how far I'd come and all I've seen. Warzone, jungles, refugee camps, language barriers, apartments, collages, and now I'm on a plane on my way to Asia with money in my pocket. And after it all, I can only credit it all to the optimism that I held on to no matter how bad things got.

The making of good decisions is, of course a prerequisite for success and it is possible that one can do a lot for them selves, but there are always people you'll meet along your path who'll help you out in all sorts of different and unexpected ways, once they see that your desire is sincere. As for my journey there are plenty of people, I owe for their support. First and for-most I have to thank the ancestors who have made it possible for many Africans to come to America without chains on their severed hands and severed feet, a scenario so common in black Americas history that it's a wonder, they aren't all crazy. In fact, the perseverance of black Americans is a story you don't hear much of, but could never really be talked enough about. I understand the rift that exists between the African American and the African community at large but when one studies the history of the violence these people have had to suffer; empathy overcomes the anger and fear that propaganda has filled our expectations with. Yes, we've had and will continue to have problems between us, but, as bad as people want to talk about black Americans, these are the very people who made America the beacon that beckons all over the world. It is incumbent on Africans to recognize that these people have been almost completely deracinated from their origin and yet, these people set the trends that the world eventually follows.

Next, I need to thank Randy Withers. Not only did he hire me as an electrical technician for Gannet Offset, but he has also been a great mentor and has in fact taught me much about my chosen field. It was an honor to work with such an open spirit of which I make sure to pass on.

I also have to thank another good friend of mine, Derrick Diesel whom I have known now for more than over seven years'. He was the kind of brother that was able to look beyond the rift that exists among African and African Americans. Like a real brother he reached out to me and we ended up becoming real good friends, hanging out at clubs, socializing and playing a lot of basketball. We met at Mystic Lake Casino, in Prior Lake, MN, where he was managing while I was a bell hop. I even convinced him to enroll in the collage that I was attending and for a while we went school together.

Derrick is very talented. Wherever he worked, he was a manager. I could always depend on him whenever I needed a job, as he was always looking out for me, giving me rides to school, he's helped me out when I was short on rent and he's always had words of encouragement for me when he knew I was struggling. *"Just hang on man, you're almost done!"* He'd tell me. I've found that most black Americans are uneasy when it comes to continental Africans, so Derricks' friendship meant a lot to me.

While Derrick and I did attend the collage of N.E.I, he had to leave before he got a chance to finish the course. I remember some of the kids at school started coming to me asking about Derrick. They knew we were always hanging around together and so I guess they expected I'd know where he was. Eventually I had to ask why were they looking for Derrick. After a brief minute of trying to make one story out of three versions, I just told them that Derrick wasn't coming back. Not wanting to hear no more of their whining, I made sure they understood that I had no idea where he was or what happened to him. I did assure them that I'd relay their message if I ever see him and I made it clear to them to keep me out of their shit. Of course Derrick and I were still the best of friends and I did tell him that the white kids at school were constantly asking me about him. He just started with that contagious laugh that always had me laughing with him. *"My bad cousin"* He'd say *"I didn't mean to get you in any shit. Those white boys came to me talking about drugs just assuming I knew all about drugs and they gave me their money because they thought I was a drug dealer, so, I figured I'd make better use out of their money, than either they or a drug dealer would. Yea, I took their money; they were throwing it away anyway. You know I've never had a problem getting a good job and have never in my life had to do anything as stupid as selling someone's drugs.* Man, Derrick had me laughing my ass off. I've seen bad drunks and schizophrenics, but the drug addicts in America are like nothing I've ever seen anywhere. I swear I've seen more dignity in the cockroaches running around in my apartment.

As I mentioned earlier, the list of people I have to thank is endless but there is one brother, Joseph Huber, AKA Semeen Reskhem, who not only helped me with this book, but he's also been like brother to me. I remember when we met some seven years ago. We were both delivery drivers for Dominoes Pizza. One day while we were at work he asked me why I wasn't delivering pizzas so I had to tell him that my car broke down and this brother, out the sky blue, from way out of left field, he actually gave me the keys to his car and let me do some driving because he understood that drivers make money from tips. From that day on we clicked like brothers and in this country that is hard to come by as most black Americans shun their Somalian brothers and sisters. Not this brother. He and his wife Bernadette have the kind of open mindedness that would make most anybody comfortable. He has the kind of positive perspective on life that I could definitely relate to. What fascinates me the most about this brother is how he tells you exactly what he thinks. No sugar coating, no beating around the bushes, just straight, real talk. Semeen, I value your friendship to the highest, not only have you been there for me when I needed you bet you've also taught me a lot. I appreciate you and Bernadette. Both of you, like so many others, will always be in my heart until my heart beats no more.

Lightning Source UK Ltd.
Milton Keynes UK
UKOW01f0704060318
318971UK00001BA/28/P